Forty Petals of the Whispering Rose

BY: ASHLEY SAPPHIRE

Healing of the Divine Rose LLC
Southington, CT 06489
www.divinerose.net

ISBN: 979-8-9864064-0-4

To My Loves Reading this,

"Tell your story,"

My spirit said

These poems were a way for me to piece together my trauma

A mirror of my own personal healing

Gifted to you

I pray that my authenticity

Gives you the strength,

Gives you the voice

Gives you the courage

To face your life experiences with compassion, grace, and higher

understanding.

The journey of writing this book has not been an easy

process over the last three years, and to those who stayed,

to those who held space, I owe this dedication:

Chris, for giving me the gift of true love.

My beautiful children, James, Vincent, Gabby, Chloe &

Amber.

My support network as I navigated this process & healed

simultaneously

Mom, Dad, Melissa, Debbie, Jim,

My dearest friends, Andrea, Kayley, Alessandra, Ellissa

The Maier Family

And all the courageous people reading this, hoping to gain

some light of empowerment through their own darkness.

Contents

—

Hope

"We don't always need to know what to do. We need to know when to surrender."

Ashley Sapphire

The rose, a symbol for eternal love
A love that never ends
Lessons taught through the unspoken love
Of mother & child

The most painful experience of my life
Bled onto the pages of this book
An act of my free will
A choice made amid adversity

We all have choices in life
I made a choice that night
One no parent ever wants
To be in the position to make

A choice that consumed me
With guilt & shame
A poison that drove me
Almost to my death
A spiritual death
As I allowed my vices to take over

We all have choices in life
I made a choice to suppress the pain
In doing so
I only hurt myself
I only hurt my loved ones
Those who wanted to help me

How does one live after

Miscarriage
    Still birth
        Child loss
            Infertility
                Abortion

A road of broken dreams

Over time illuminating
Predetermined action
Or
Free will

Neither right
nor wrong

Pushing through adversity
We decide one over what
Would be unacceptable

We all have the power in life
I desire to live
I prefer to endure
Allowing the death of my spirit
To rebirth who I was born to be

The Divine using the story written here
To highlight your path to freedom
Freedom from the shame, the guilt
Of the decisions you have made
Decisions that brought you to this moment
To be the light in your life
As well as another's

Science
Quantum physics
Spirituality
Religion

All attempting to say the same thing
That we are all connected
Through Universal Law
Collective consciousness
The creator's unconditional love

The root of healing is founded in love
Anything outside of that

Is not truth

I extend this bouquet of roses to you
That whatever you may be struggling with
You shall forgive yourself
You shall forgive those who have hurt you
As you allow the love of the Universe, the Divine, the
Creator
To move through your spirit

Blossoming like a rose yourself
Opening your petals
To the radiant warmth of sunshine
Inviting in a faith
That roots you to the security of Gaia

All is as it should be
Says the laws of nature
Allowing the rain to wash away
The petals that have begun to wilt
Wilting away the feelings of
Shame
       Guilt
            Bitterness
                  Resentment

All of that which prevents you
From fully blooming

Like the eternal rose
That you are

The Tragedy

"Suffering is necessary, until you realize it is unnecessary."

Eckhart Tolle

"This is going to be too painful for you to feel."

I remember that night so vividly, often in fragmented
pieces
Fragmented pieces of that night
Somehow jumbled in with my present moment.
It can be so confusing to live between these two worlds
My mind flipping through the channels
Unable to decide where to land
Do I pick a psychological horror film
Like Silence of the Lambs
Or put Netflix on repeat to tune everything out

How could you ever forget the night your child died
The memory always begins with me
Slowly sitting on the edge of my couch
The couch of the sunroom
Designed to be my space of peace

I need to process what just happened
Hands gripping my knees
Rubbing my gray leggings

Back and forth
Back and forth
Staring at the hardwood floor, zoning out

My subconscious begins to take over
'This is going to be too painful for you to feel"
My subconscious tells me.
It's time to dissociate, Ashley.

I begin to lose touch with my body
Floating just a few inches off the ground
A tingling sensation gripping my legs
Shooting to the top of my head
Everything frozen over
The only way to move away from this pain

I just went to the bathroom.

POP

A trickling sensation followed
Stunned by what just happened
I find myself staring ahead at the mirror
Like a deer caught in headlights

The blood begins to rush from my face
My beautiful, olive skin
Replaced with the coloration of an ominous spirit

What…
The fuck…
Was that…

As I realize I am holding my breath
I let go
A helium balloon
Suddenly losing the tie
That keeps it whole

Not my first pregnancy
I know exactly what that sound was
But it cannot be that
God wouldn't do this to me

A gaping pit in my stomach
Makes space for the movement of my heart
As the devastation of my reality moves
Through my physical body

I try to pull up my pants
I can't feel anything anymore
Was I even touching my legs?
A slow morphine drip

My body naturally releasing hormones
To protect me from the trifecta of pain
Now spreading through my body
I am able to organize my thoughts

I am five months pregnant
This should not be happening to me.
What kind of mother doesn't know she's in labor?
A bad mother, I tell myself.

Just a few days before,
I questioned the signs of labor
Second guessing myself
Yet guided to seek support
The on-call doctor treated me
Like I was wasting his time

A sigh resounding from the other end of the phone
"There is nothing wrong with you."
A callousness rolling off his tongue
Rushing me off the phone
Prompting me into a void
A chain of futility seizing me

Crazy first-time mother.
I'm not, though?
So much for self-advocating.
How did I not know those were contractions?
I was in pain all weekend.
I nested all day Sunday.
How did I not realize I was nesting?
What kind of mother am I?
What kind of person am I?

I continue to stare at the floor,

Shame overshadowing the experience
As the self-criticism flows through my veins
Unbearable guilt
Now rationalizing what is unfolding

I asked Donnie to take the kids to the other room.
They didn't need to hear this call.
I intuitively knew what was going to happen next
I couldn't have them see that

Donnie doesn't pressure me for a why
Why I need the kids to leave the room
Why my eyes are full of tears
Why I look like I've just seen a ghost

He just does it.
He never asks questions.
I always thought this meant we were a team.
I have realized over time, he just didn't care to ask
At least that's how it has come to feel

When he came back, I looked up at him, my eyes welling
up with tears

"I think I'm in labor.

"You came at the wrong time, Chloe"

I thought to myself,
Over the course of my pregnancy
Too many times to count

And now,
Here we are,
Sitting on this couch.
Coming at the wrong time.

This is all my fault
Everything is always my fault
I just can't do anything right

I call my doctor to let her know what is happening
I can barely hear my own voice
I call my mom to let her know what is happening
She's on her way over
I text my sister to let her know what is happening
She gets in her car to leave Michigan

Like a robot
Simply moving through the motions
Disconnected from my reality
Sitting on this damn couch I wanted so badly

This was the perfect house
It would fix all of our problems
The indignation continuing
All the ways I have failed

I was so angry
For so long
After finding out I was pregnant.

So much so
I pretended that I wasn't pregnant
Until I couldn't pretend anymore.

I was trying to find the courage to file for divorce.

I felt trapped with Donnie

The mystery that emanated from his shadows
What are you hiding, Donnie?
He always joked
"You are the light. I am the darkness."
"My own personal heroin."

This was no joke though
It was a trauma bond mirror
Illuminating our toxicity
Fueled back & forth
Through the infinite cycle
Of a venomous love

His eyes tell the story of his trauma
The betrayal wounds
The darkness of the circles under his eyes,
Not from exhaustion
But his ever-present rage

His contempt for women,
How could he ever experience vulnerability
When the one who gave him life
Made him feel like the red-headed step-child

He always knew something was missing
Spending our marriage piecing together
The reasoning behind why he couldn't connect with his
mother

The woman who punched him on our wedding day
And asked his wife,
"Why did you marry that piece of shit?"

We never stood a chance

"You can fix him."
"Your love will heal him."
"It's not his fault he is this way."
"This is why he needs you in his life."

"Show him what unconditional love is."

All I was doing
Was trying to control him
His healing
Hurting him
Rather than helping him

Over time, I stopped trying
Our marriage highlighting my codependency
Enmeshed through trauma bonding
And the resentment that came with failed caretaking

I had no idea this was happening
Escapism came naturally as a result
A bottle of wine a night
A pack of cigarettes a night
Fantasizing about a different life.

And then a positive pregnancy test
On our wedding anniversary
What a sick joke, Universe
It just confirmed that I was meant to be

Stuck
Miserable
Alone
Sad
Unheard

The anger moved through me like a raging fire
I resented my baby.

This baby was going to be the reason
I would remain bound & shackled to this mother fucker
For yet another lifetime
Our wedding song
1,000 Years

A vow of misery birthed through my fears & insecurities
Limited by my beliefs of *this is all I deserve*

Why should *I* have better?

I had to stay on the shelf with the other misfit toys
Until it was time to make him look like the perfect man
I had to stay
4 kids, no more career, and the opinion of family & friends
My fate was sealed

"The neighbor is on her way over now." Donnie *says*
I snap back to the present moment
Looking up at him, standing over me, I whisper
"Okay."

He always stands over me like that,
No matter how much I express the discomfort it produces
With him being so much bigger than me
Towering over me
He still does it

Leaving the room as fast as he came in
I tell myself it's time to get up
I grab the armrest on the side of the couch
Slowly pulling myself up to a standing position

I gently take one step forward
What I was avoiding with the extreme care
Now irrelevant

Like a fire hydrant when the pressure is finally released
I look down at the puddle on the ground
My hands suddenly feel sticky
Sweat dripping down my forehead
The sound of my heart beating
Pulsating my ear drums

NO, NO, NO
Tears begin to roll down my face
This cannot be happening
I knew this was going to happen
But this cannot be it for me

The screeching sound
Of a barn owl
AHHHHHHHHHHHHHHH
NOOOOOOOO!
GOD NOOOOOOO!

The pressure of an elephant sitting on my chest
Air siphoned from my lungs
The word heartbreak not metaphorical in this moment
My heart cracks as my mind brings to balance

The pain that my body was trying to protect me from
The agony of what I intuitively already knew to be true
Was unfolding in this moment
Faster than my mind could process

Frozen
Standing there
The screaming won't stop
My legs are bent
I put out my hands
Balancing myself so as not to fall
This will make it stop

Suddenly, Blake and I lock eyes in the doorway
A moment frozen in time

How long has he been standing there?
What did he see?
What did he hear?
What does he think is happening?
Why can't I say anything to him?

My poor son
We're both afraid
I stop screaming
"Get your father NOW."

Where the hell is Donnie?

"It's a girl!"

The date is February 4, 2019
Trapped in a lucid dream
Just three days past the most beautiful dream
I could have ever had

A dream signifying
Chloe & I had finally connected
That I had let my resentments go

Of her being the ball & chain
That bound me to a life with the parasite I call her father
Surrendering to God's plan for my life

Finally, experiencing a mother's joy
Over having another baby
For Chloe's arrival
Preparing Sophia's room for two girls
A dream confirming that I was having a baby girl

What would come after, would come.
I am still going to file for divorce
I can love this child
While still wanting to break free

I just knew I wanted you
I just knew I adored you

I quickly snapped out of my daze
Animal instincts kicking in

Run! I need to run!
I need to get to the hospital,
I need them to stop this labor,
I need to save my baby!

Every step forward
The loss continues

Followed by a whimper
Simply trying to get to the door

What is keeping her alive...
What is keeping her breathing...
Leaving me faster than I know what to do with

How much time does she have?
Is she even alive?
If I stop running, it will stop coming out of me
But if I stop running, I can't get to the car

I don't know where the kids are
Blake?
Liam?
Sophia?

All I see now, is the kitchen door
My eyes fixate on the open door
Visible from my living room

Drenched
As if I left the car window open
In a torrential downpour

My neighbor comes through the kitchen door,
As I barrel outside, finally reaching the door
"Everything is going to be okay," she says.
"No. No it's actually not."
I yell...

Shaking my head
My hands over my face
I look up at Donnie standing in the driveway
Waiting for me
Why was he outside this whole time?

"This baby will have great purpose"

I don't remember getting in the car
I do remember the piercing silence as we drove to the
hospital
Pressing my head against the glass
Trying to find some light in the sky

The moon, unable to reflect any light in this phase
Has me surrendering blindly into the purpose of all of this
A customer of mine had said just earlier that day
"This baby will have great purpose."

I didn't understand what he meant then
And I still don't understand in this moment
What I do understand is the emptiness of the night sky
The total absence of light
Is embodying exactly how I feel in this moment
Empty and alone

Desperately searching for a star
Some glimmer of hope
Some sign that all would be well
But all it did was remind me how hopeless my life was

*"This is the best it will ever be for you Ashley. You should
be grateful."*

My inner critic was such a miserable bitch

I never noticed my surroundings
Until I met Ryan
Such as the way the sun setting
Reflects onto the leaves
Painting them in shades of crimson gold & fire orange
Opening my eyes to so much about life
Teaching me to slow down
And soak in the beauty of all that surrounds us
Just a bit more

I keep looking at the dreary, black sky

Ensnared with gray clouds
All I could do, was think of him
Maybe the thought of him was the bright star in the sky
I was so desperately looking for
God, planting the seed of the good things to come for me

Thinking of his gentleness
Was easier than thinking about
What was happening
My escapism was disrupted by the sudden ringing of my
phone

I jump at the sound, quickly answering
He-hello!?
My voice cracks
My throat feels so dry
I need water

*"Ashley, it's Dr. Ward. I'm at the hospital. Come through
the emergency room and we'll get you right into a room to
check the baby."*

"My...my water broke..."
I can barely muster any words
Tears interrupting

I don't know what else to say
My throat is beginning to close
"I'll be getting off the exit soon."
I hang up
I just want to get to her
She's the only one I trust right now
It was 6:16 p.m.
I will be experiencing new meaning for my life.

"I'm in labor."

What felt like an hour-long drive
Was only fifteen minutes
As Donnie pulls up to the emergency room
I am jumping out of the car
I cannot wait for him to stop
I have to get inside

Unable to feel my legs
Against the ground
I floated through those double doors
My spirit ahead of my body
Maybe this is what that prayer,
"Footprints in the Sand" is all about
Was God carrying me through this?

It felt like I was just going to a regular check up
Or maybe that was my maladaptive way of keeping me safe
Tuning out the hell on earth of what was happening
As I almost feel normal now

Able to walk without disruption
What happened in the house, now a distant memory
Everything has stopped
I am convinced Chloe is dead
Nothing left but an empty shell

I can't seem to wake from this nightmare
As it transitions from one scene to the next
I rush into the emergency room
Just to crash into a long line of people

Of course
This would be my luck
I stood there,
Asking God,
Why?
Humiliated, standing for all to see
Trying not to scream

Hurry the fuck up
Can't you tell it's an emergency?

My pants are completely soaked
The evidence covering my ass
How can they not see what I've been through?
Why am I so invisible?
Why can't anyone see me?

I feel Donnie brush behind me, suddenly
I saw him hand the valet the keys
Why did it take him so long to meet me in the waiting area?
Why wouldn't he think to rush in with his wife?
I am in labor with his daughter

Why does he keep disappearing?
Doesn't he realize how serious this is?
Why am I always left asking, where the fuck is Donnie?

"Would you like us to get you a wheelchair?"
Someone finally asks.
All I can muster to say…
"Yes."

As the nurse pushes me to the elevator
She hits the button for the 4th Floor.

Labor & Delivery
Here we come
A moment usually so full of joy
Now, just absolute fear
Fully knowing this is not going to end well

"Her heartbeat is 170!"

The moment that I arrive on the Labor & Delivery floor
The moment I enter the exam room
I begin to accept that this nightmare
Is in fact my reality

What are the odds of her living through this?
All I can think about
Is how I am going to deliver my baby
At just five months pregnant

I suddenly notice that this is not
A normal delivery room
And the panic of the unfamiliar
Sets in

I lay down on the bed
Staring right up at the ceiling
The doctors and nurses rush in
Hooking me up to monitor after monitor

Held hostage to the situation
Unable to move
Processing everything long after it happens
While everyone sprints around me
A copiousness of chatter, everyone talking over each other

As if someone hit fast forward on the VCR
Muting the bustling of activity that swirls around me
Everyone moving voraciously in the room
Motionless
In space, in time

She's moving!
And we're back

Things now moving at a normal pace.
Sound returns
Faith restored

Exhaling a deep sigh of relief
Right down to my stomach
I had been holding everything in
Since this all started it seemed

She is alive
There are no signs of distress
She is healthy
She is a girl!
My dream was right!

I place my hands on my belly,
Nurturing her
Talking to her
Mommy loves you so much!

For just a moment, I have peace
Like watching a sunset
Attempting to understand
The miracle behind the beautiful blend of colors
How no single sunset can look the same

I am able to smile,
Closing my eyes to connect with her,
The tears gently brushing down my face
Salt penetrating the pursing of my lips
My whole body embracing the joy of this moment
As the feeling returns to my legs

God really did hear my prayers, I realize
All of the smiles in the room quickly shift as my doctor
says,
"Ashley, you've lost 2/3 of your amniotic fluid."
I know. It's all over the floors of my house, my clothes
I think sarcastically
I change into the gown they give me
As I settle into what must come next
I have to go to the bathroom first

As I am walking
Something tells me to look down

Suspended in fear
All of the blood leaving my face
Again
I look back at Donnie
Standing in the doorway

My eyes well up with tears
There's a trail of blood as I walk
My ears start ringing
My hands begin to clam up
I suddenly feel cold
My legs buckle from the weight
Of this never-ending agonizing experience

As I fall, I catch myself just over the toilet
Burying my head into my arms
I begin to sob uncontrollably
While Donnie runs to get a nurse

It's too late

"Please God, don't take her from me."
Was the only prayer I could muster up
"Please God, I will do anything. Just don't take her from me."

"If we stop the labor, you both could die."

I look at Chloe moving around on the ultrasound
My doctors intern checks how far dilated I am
The pain is agonizing
She tries again
I scream this time
"Get my doctor!"

They inform us that I have an ascending infection
That's what caused my water to break
An ascending infection?
They can't tell us anything beyond that

Donnie and I had tried to be intimate a week earlier
Interrupted by me bawling my eyes out
My body completely resisted the idea
How is any of this even possible?

Not convinced on the decision that had to be made
A NICU doctor came to meet us
Her chances of survival were quite low
Stopping my labor would cause us both to become septic

I look to Donnie
I don't know what to do
He stares back at me
This feels like an abortion
Despite the fact that I'm in labor

My doctor reassures me it is not
But we're people of faith?
Maybe we should trust God to get us through this
The fear of dying though
Of leaving my babies without a mother

This was something neither of us could justify with our
faith
And the decision is made
A decision I never thought I would be faced with
There is a chance I could see her first breath, though

I am holding onto that glimmer of hope
Maybe, just maybe, I will have a few minutes with her
I opt out of receiving pain medication

I just want to see Chloe alive
I don't want her to be groggy from the medications
I want her to be fully alert
To hear that first newborn cry
To kiss her on those beautiful baby lips
To look in her big, oval eyes
And tell her how much mommy *does love her.*

Time to move to a delivery room
"Father Monroe is on his way"
I feel comfort in knowing my priest will be with me
However, his presence does reiterate
That this delivery won't be like the others
The winter solstice of my life story
Now entering the longest night of my life

"I need everyone to leave the room."

I lay there gazing at the neutral wall
The color triggers no emotion
The room feels as cold and empty
As I do in this moment

My contractions feel like cramps
This is always how it begins
Yet, for some reason
I assume that because she is smaller
My labor will be less intense
That couldn't have been farther from the truth

I look up from my bed
And catch myself staring at a large, white clock on the wall
Reinforcing how institutionalized the room feels

As I sit up straight,
I drape my hands over my lap
Donnie sits tucked in the back, right corner
Behind me

He can't handle this kind of stuff
Always waiting for my direction
This time
I don't even have a sense of one

My mom is straight ahead
Under the large, white clock
Reminding me that I am sitting in a prison right now

I continue to stare
As the big hand just ticks
Each minute that goes by
All of us
Sitting there in total silence
Like my other deliveries
But somewhat different

This time

Anticipating death
Rather than life

The excruciating pain endured
Just so I can hear her cry
Just once
No pain killers
I can do this for my daughter

As I'm sitting here
I feel numb
A body void of any spirit
What is there to think or feel
My life ending the moment
I entered those hospital doors

Just biding my time
So much pain
Yet still so numb

My eyes brighten with hope as my priest walks in
The energy shifting like clouds amidst a storm
A ray of light shining through
Peace amidst the chaos

He grabs a chair, and sits by my side
He doesn't start citing scripture
He just sits with me
In that moment, it feels like it is just him and I

I begin to feel so much pressure
I think I have to use the bathroom
I look down
Nope

Never have I seen anything like this before
What is wrong?
Why is this happening?

The nurse comes with me to the bathroom
As she walks by, the scent of her lotion

Triggers something within me
The scent is familiar
Coconut
A symbol of liberation
From the constraints of the ego
Engulfing me with a fleeting sense of optimism

"I'm going to place this here just in case you push too hard."

Uh, what?
Just in case I deliver her?
I didn't know that was possible
Panic begins to set in again
Though I don't think it ever left

How do I do this?
I sit
And then I stand up
I can't do this

The discomfort
The pressure
I have to try
Scared to push
I sit there

No, I can't do this
I can't deliver her in the toilet
A little trickles out
I don't feel any relief

I can't wrap my head around
The sudden fear of delivering her
Right then and there
I won't get up to use the bathroom anymore
I will just deal with it

I'm getting so uncomfortable
There is so much pressure
The pain begins to hasten

It is just like every other delivery I have had
Her size is irrelevant to the feeling of the contractions
What was I thinking?

I cry out in pain
My contractions are finally at the point
Face beginning to wince
As I brace the tightness in my belly
Arching my back to aid with the pain
A desire to cross my legs consuming me

Pressure developing
It's time to push
I feel so scared
Not so much from the pain
But what is to come next

Will Chloe survive this?
Breathe
Don't hold your breath
Breathe through the pain
I tell myself

They keep checking me
I'm bleeding too much
I suddenly feel so embarrassed
Why am I embarrassed?

I don't want Father Monroe to leave me
But I can't have him see this
See me like this
I'm only 4 cm dilated
My body wants to deliver her
But there's not enough room

She's in the birth canal
"You have to stop pushing."
But if I stop pushing
She'll die
She'll have no oxygen

"But, you could hurt her if you push too hard. You have to wait."

I can feel her just sitting there
She's stuck
I lace my fingers over my chest
Attempting to stop the labor, I cross my legs

How do I tell my body to stop
What it naturally wants to do?
I ask for my priest to come back
My eyes welling
I grip the sides of the bed
I can't find the words
But he knows what I mean
Why? Tell me why?

My face twisting in agony
How can my heart hurt more
Than what my body is going through?

He puts his hand on my shoulder
I roll my head to the side
The tears flood my face
As the dam breaks inside of me

The physical pain
An aching heart
Complete helplessness

Where are you God? Why have you left me?

"You're 8 cm. You can start pushing now."

I don't even know how much time has passed
I stopped looking at the clock
I was so focused on stopping the urge to push

Begging
Pleading
With this so-called
Higher power of a God

I am trying to understand why this is happening
What is the purpose behind all of this?
The discomfort
The fidgeting
Trying to keep her from moving further down

Holding my breath
The warmth of my tears
Slowly streaming down my face
The taste of salt as they hit my lips

My doctor left me to be with another mom
Delivering a full-term baby
Her intern is now responsible for my delivery
The sound is starting to fade out again

I close my eyes
And as I open them
I look to my left
My nurse is at her station typing something

I look straight ahead
I can see the intern talking to me
I can't hear anything, though

I push and I see the nervous look on her face
No Chloe

But something
She looks scared
Pretending like everything is okay

None of this feels okay
The nurse comes over to help
The intern puts her hand on my belly
I push again

The sudden paleness in her face
As if she saw a ghost
No Chloe
I should feel scared right now
Is what her face is telling me

Yet I don't
I don't feel alive
Just another object
On this delivery table

Maybe I'm dying
Maybe we will get to die together
The idea of escaping this miserable existence
This way
Feels right

Able to hear the noise around me again
We need you NOW!
The intern rushes out of the room
My doctor needs help with the other mom

My condition is not of any concern
Simply leaving me there like that
Why did they leave me?
How could they just leave me like this?

I don't understand
I'm in the middle of delivering a baby
Frantically looking around
Why don't I matter?
The nurse goes back to her station to type
Where is the care? The comfort?
I feel the urge to push
I look at Donnie to my right

The tears lodged in my throat
Be strong
Or let it all out
My face pleading
Just for someone to come help me

Donnie finally stands up
He doesn't know what to do
If I don't understand what's happening
How could he?

I look back at the clock
Something in me tells me to push
She's finally moving
A sense of relief passes through my body

Breathing out
I look up at Donnie
"She's coming!"
My voice sounds more like a squeak

I look back at the clock

It's 3:27 a.m.
One more push

The sound of Chloe hitting the table
Stops me in all that I was thinking
Eyes widening at the realization
No
Way

I look at my nurse
"I just delivered her."
The nurse doesn't move
Maybe she didn't hear me?
Why can't anyone hear me?
Donnie starts to move towards my feet
I go to say it again
My fists are clenched
Squeezing the sheets in my hand
I am ready to explode on these people

When she starts to walk over
Why was there no urgency?
Why don't I matter?
Why did I just deliver my baby
Myself?

A crime scene
My nurse, the detective
Observing the evidence
Of a something that should have never happened
She drops the sheet

I feel so dirty
Chloe is still under the sheet
Rage
Disgust
We don't deserve this
I go to lift the sheet myself
One of us is still alive here

The nurse and I lock eyes

She begins to walk back over to me

2.5.19

Recording time of birth
3:30 a.m.
Recording time of death
3:30 a.m.
Was far more important
Than the baby that was left for dead on the table.

"You almost died. I was close to taking the uterus out."

I feel myself floating away
I hope I'm dying.
The only thought I can think in this moment

Doctors chose another mom in labor
Over me
Anxiously running from
What I was enduring through

Everyone always chooses someone else
But never me
Chloe's chances of survival were less
So I deserved less care

The desertion I felt
Delivering her by myself
The sound of her hitting the table

She didn't matter as much
Because of the presumption
That she would be dead

I don't matter to anyone
Nor did my daughter
Drifting farther away
A sudden warmth blankets over me

The ceiling begins to move
I can't focus my eyes
I feel drunk
The room is spinning
Is God answering my prayer?

I asked him to not take her from me
So, is He taking us both away to Him?

Will I finally have freedom
From this painful life?
My doctor and the intern rush in

Why can't I hear anything?
The sound keeps going in and out
Poor connection
Is this what floating between two worlds feels like?

"We have to deliver the placenta."
The intern says
It's not over!

The nurse is cleaning up Chloe
Why did they just interrupt me?
I felt like I was high
I felt like I was finally free

The intern pushes on my belly
The placenta is stuck
There is so much resistance
The pain is unbearable

It's as if
My body knew
It wasn't supposed to be this way
More pain
As she removes it herself

It's not supposed to be this way

Chapter 2

"The secret to life is to die before you die."

Eckhart Tolle

"She looks just like Sophia."

The nurse hands me Chloe
As my hands touch the nurses'
I can't help but feel so afraid

She is so tiny, so fragile
Dainty
Barely weighing one pound

I stare at her face
With the simple desire
To never forget
What she looks like

She has Donnie's pointy ears, his toes
She has my chin, my jawline
Sophia's twin
Her eyes are closed
But I feel
In my heart
She has beautiful, round eyes
Just like her siblings

The size of a Barbie doll
A mother's love
Only sees perfection
Even in this moment
Of facing her death

Swaddled in a beautiful blanket

Blue gems encased in silk
A color for sadness
The sky-blue inciting hope
The silk gentle to touch
On my trembling skin

I sob uncontrollably
Kissing her forehead
Fostering safety
Between mother and child

Donnie snaps a picture
Tears uniting our faces
A final goodbye
A moment I never thought I'd experience
Farewell before it even began

I hand her to Donnie
He doesn't seem to know what to do
But he sits on the bed next to me
Holding her
His eyes scanning her small body

Hard to read his face
The tremble in his voice
As he sings his made-up song
"My baby...yeah..."

When he looks up
His eyes are glossed over
Holding back the water
Beginning to fill in his eyes
Never quite releasing

The pain that stirs
I reflect on what this moment should comprise
Relief to finally have my pregnancy be over
Replaced with the bliss of holding my baby

How do I connect with my dead baby?
"Spend as much time as possible with her."
Something inside of me says.

Her skin begins to turn white
As I hold her

It's time to put her back in her crib
To keep her body cool
When she is cool enough
I can hold her again

It's amazing how
Regardless of circumstances
We innately know what to do
As mothers

After an hour
It's time to baptize her
My priest begins
The Catholic ritual
He's supposed to be holding mass in two hours

He hasn't slept all night
He's been here the whole time
With me
He holds such a love for my family

Father Monroe gently takes Chloe from my arms
And cradles her against his chest
He looks down at her
Tenderly touching her face

My direct line to God
The wrinkling up of his face
A drought now over
As the rain barrel begins to fill
He stood shocked silence
Eyes dumbfounded
I imagine they didn't cover this in seminary school
The feelings are ever-present

No words can be articulated
Just universal understanding
Of how painful this shared moment is

So tiny
So perfect
Father Monroe begins to cry
Looking away from Chloe
And up at me
Eyes welling up

"How could God let something like this happen?"
There is no answer.
No one has an answer.
And even the look
On Father Monroe's face
Suggests he poses the same question

"Why did you take her from me, God?"

"You can't leave until funeral arrangements are set."

I sit upright in my bed
Physically uncomfortable
Afraid to fall asleep
The reality of waking
Is one without Chloe

The daze of
Dissociation
As if I was a junkie
After chasing the dragon
My body is here
Yet there is an absence of consciousness
I might as well be dead

I sluggishly roll my head to the left
As the sun begins to come up
Rays of orange and gold begin to break the surface
Over the city buildings

Donnie is going to the diner to get us breakfast
The one we ate at
Every Sunday
After church
A ham & cheese omelet
Whole wheat toast
Hashbrowns
Enough to make me feel alive for a moment

He needs to clear his head
And I need comfort food

Chloe is sleeping
Silently
In her bassinet

I hear footsteps coming down the hall
Through my room

Another new face

I am just a specimen

To be observed, poked & prodded
By the wide array of medical staff
That finds my tragedy
Enthralling

Where was this attention
When I was delivering
The footsteps identify themselves
As a cold & callous social worker
Simply making her rounds

I don't even know how to feel right now
All I want to do is leave
To be with my other children
To hug them so tight
And never let go
To tell them how much I love them

I want my own bed
My home
Rather than the place
Where a piece of me just died

The social worker can see that I am upset
She tries to talk to me
"My daughter is dead! What the fuck do you want to talk about?"
I scream at her

All I can think about are Blake, Liam and Sophia
I need to get home to my other children
They went to school this morning
After watching what happened
I have to make sure they are okay
The social worker slowly gets up from her chair
The sound of my voice won't stop

Donnie returns

As it is time for Chloe to be taken
I pick her up
Burrowing my face in her little body
I don't ever want to forget this moment

I cry and cry and cry
No, this just can't be
This can't be the last time I get to hold my sweet Chloe
This all feels so unfair

"I'm so sorry."

The only words I can spare
Endless sobbing
My lungs working so hard
They begin to cave
I can't breathe

Anxiety spinning in my stomach
Turning over to vomit
I look up, around the room

"Just one more minute, please."

She's gone.

Laying there lifeless
The sound begins to fade
I can see Donnie on his phone
And I feel myself drifting away

How could there be life after this?

"No one comes between me & my children."

I begin to change into the clothes
My mother-in-law brought to the hospital
An olive-green tank top
And soft, gray sweat that fit comfortably around me

I'm in shock at her support
As she has caused more harm
Than help
In all our time together

Sitting on the edge of the bed
I slip one leg into each pant leg
The physical discomfort of postpartum
Typically balanced out with the joyous experience
Of carrying your baby to the car

Fixing the brand-new infant car seat
And gently placing your sleepy baby
Being so careful
Not to rub the umbilical cord
A gentle kiss on the forehead
And gratitude to be experiencing
The miracle of life

"Ashley!"
I hear Donnie's voice
Snapping me back to reality
What do I have to do, to get her back?

Pulling up my pants
Signifies the end
Of this hospital stay

It isn't supposed to be this way
The nurse comes in, ready to wheel me out
Discharging me from the prison of this nightmare
I shut my eyes as
The four walls begin closing in on me
Palms sweaty

Chest heavy
Room spinning
I don't want to throw up again
I squeeze my eyes tighter together

I need to just get out of here

Another stop at the nurse's station
To remove the bracelet
Connecting me to my Chloe

I'm leaving the maternity ward
Without a baby

Donnie continues to push me down the hallway
When the social worker catches up to us

"You really should consider staying longer."
Donnie tells her to get away from us
"I need to get home to my kids!"
I screech

Arriving on the first floor
Windows for a ceiling
The sun is beaming down
As we move through the corridor

My eyes focused straight ahead
A daze of some sort
Did they give me something before I left?
Completely out of control
Rapidly brought back in
With a single shot of lithium

People on both sides of me
Time has stopped
But I am still moving

Everyone is staring at me
I can feel it

Look at that mom
Without her baby
What happened?

An empty shell
How does a mother go on
After something like that

I ask Donnie to take me to the park
The valet brought my car up
All I had to do was get in
And forget this ever happened

We stop at the bodega
Incense
Cigarettes
Exactly what I need
This was how he knew to express his love
His way of comforting me

Vodka and cigarettes
What made his mom nice again
Wine and cigarettes
To keep his wife happy

We stop at the park
Where our boys first played baseball
As we walk to the bench
Overlooking the field

My house slippers sink into the mud
The cold, wet sensation
Barely phases me

I am determined to get to the bench
Despite feeling stuck
Here in this spot
One foot
After the other

The much-needed cigarette
Tastes so terrible
After months of not smoking

I don't care at all
The simple act of
Sitting
Dazing
Puffing

It's so cloudy out
The despair of the sky
In sync with my emotions
Grief, sadness, desolation
Moving through me
But not out of me

It seems even Heaven mourns this tragic loss

How does one survive something like this?

"Your sister didn't make it last night."

We made it home just in time
To get Blake and Liam off the bus
I walk out to the end of the driveway
Smiling as I see their excitement
In seeing me home

I knew I had to leave the hospital
Finally trusting my gut
Honoring my needs

I walk them inside
Donnie and mom are sitting at the table
We have them sit down next to each other
And I take my place next to Donnie

Leaning in, I grab each of their hands
And break the news to them
"Your sister didn't make it."

They're so young
I'm unsure they fully comprehend what has happened
Blake bursts out into tears
All he wanted was to hold Chloe
Liam sits there silently
Not knowing how to react

One of the biggest things I regret
Is not having the kids meet her
I thought I was protecting them

But I would give anything to have that
One picture
Of my children
Together

To allow them the opportunity
To have a physical connection to her

Blake runs to his room crying
I don't know what to do
How do I comfort him?
When this doesn't even feel real to me?

Liam seems confused
Slips out of his chair
And follows Blake

I sit there at the table
Helpless
Hopeless

Donnie goes outside to have a cigarette
And I just sit there and think

Every dream I had
Of Sophia and her sister
Playing dolls
Dressing up
Fighting over clothes and shoes

Gone
Never to be had
Losing her is hard
But how do I move through the rest of my life
Knowing all I had dreamed of
Was gone?

"You should be used to this by now."

Everyone is sleeping
I am wide awake
Laying on the couch in my sunroom
Avoiding the spot where it all happened

It's been an entire 24 hours
How has a whole day gone by?
I just want to forget
All of this ever happened

Donnie sleeps soundly
How can he sleep?
I can feel this fire stirring
As I realize my body begins to make
What is needed to tend to a newborn baby
How does my body not yet know
That the baby it's built to carry & feed
Is no longer here?

My voice, desperate to be heard
I scream out in pain
Tears flowing down my face
My stomach clenching in torment
As my body convulses
The stabbing sensation in my chest

Is this my fault
Because I resented her?
I allowed myself to love her
How could this have happened?

None of this real
I can't make it stop
I can't move from where I am
I try to cry out for Donnie
But he doesn't come
I know I'm screaming
So why doesn't he hear me?

I feel like I'm dying
I can't wipe the tears away fast enough
Blurring my vision
Like pointless windshield wipers
Amidst a hurricane
I am always alone

Why, God?
If you are real, why?
Why did you have to give me this life?

Pain my backstory
What is the point in even being here
Why must I feel this
I can't handle this physical pain
How does my body hurt
When my heart is what aches
I feel crazy

What do you have
To be so angry about?

"I'm so sorry, Chloe."

I sit on the cold ground
My hand next to where she is to be buried
I'm not ready to leave
To say good-bye
A crow caws
I look up at him
Sitting in the tree
The sign of death

I have always been drawn to crows
Maybe he is here for me?

Even when things
Are out of our control
We naturally internalize
Shame
Blame

Why do I keep apologizing
Could have done something different
Stopped this from happening

How do you ever say good-bye to your child
It's unnatural
We bring them into this world
To grow into what they were always meant to be
Not to watch them die
Before our time

My sister holds me during the calling hours
As Sophia runs up to her sister's coffin
The cross hanging above
Reassurance of eternal life
Kneeling
Praying

How did someone so young
Know exactly what to do
That innate desire to bond
With your sister

My sister and I never grew up together
The connection of sisters
So special to experience
We met a few years prior
Yet had such a profound love
For one another
All I wanted for Sophia
Now she will never get to have

My dad begins to tear up
I see him from the corner of my eye
A man that never cries
Fully understands the severity of
What's happening

As we gather to enter the church
My brother-in-law
Carries her little coffin
Another powerful masculine
Moved to tears
By the tragedy
That hit our family

I move through the motions
As if I have done this before
Taking my seat
In a spot that wasn't mine

We attend mass here
Every Sunday
Now attending
A funeral

This should never have happened
No words to describe the injustice
Felt through the agony of the experience
I will never be able to come back
To this place

Sophia keeps running
Up and down the aisles
Anxiety moving through me
I smell the presence of rosemary
Nervous
People are already watching me
Why can't I just focus on grieving?

Blake keeps crying
I console him
My attention is everywhere
But this funeral

I can feel eyes on my back
Lasers burning through the walls
That I put up years ago

A spectacle
To be pitied
Why am I always a victim?

My soul craves so much more than this
Pain, suffering, tragedy
Mass is over
How did that happen?

They are moving her casket already
Jumping up
My legs not grounded
I fall into the pew

Gasping for air
My hand on my chest

The room is spinning
I look up
Everyone halfway down the aisle
I look back at the cross
Christ hanging there
"Why have you forsaken me?"

Even in His darkest hour
He cried out in pain
At the absence of the almighty Father

I snap out of my daze
Beginning to run
Weeping profusely

Despite this almost being over
It feels like something has just begun
I can see the light
Beaming through the church doors

Get me the fuck out of here!

"Chloe's sunset."

Arriving back home
The cars line the street
Consumed by overwhelm
I already begin to count down the hours
Before everyone leaves

The reception is at my home
This should have made things easier
But my safe place being full of people
I have nowhere to run

Grieving my daughter
I step through the gates
Leading to my backyard
I scan the yard for where I can hide
Darting for the shed
Donnie trying to keep up with me
Unsure of the direction I'm moving

The wind blows the swing as I run past
No one will find me here
I just need to find my breath
That's all

All of this is happening so fast
While also not happening fast enough
Donnie lights up a cigarette
And hands it to me

Silence consumes us
The shed fills with smoke
The cotton on my dress
Soaking up the scent
Of poison

I finish my cigarette
And slowly make my way
Toward the house
Donnie continuing to trail behind
I'm not sure what he's thinking
We haven't been able to talk
What an awkward dance we share
In the presence of one another

How do you continue to live
When death devours you
Part of me
Was buried
With my little girl

Something within
Tells me to look up
Turkey vultures
Soar above
The presence of death
So ominous
Seeping through my pores
As I sweat in the anticipation
Of speaking to people

The birds circle
My grief
So profound
I emanate the scent of death
As they tell me to let go

How could any of this
Be part of God's plan?

"Her Death, the Only Memory I Now Have"

Chloe Susan
Once a dream
Now just a distant memory
Occasionally revisited by the triggers
Or the contents of your memory box

The only memories I will ever have with you
Encompassed in your death
I open this box of your things
To feel as close as is humanly possible
Never quite filling the void
That exists in this mother's heart

A cute, little birth announcement
An attempt to remind me
That I am a mother
That your life is as cherished
As your brothers & sisters

Laid on cardstock, the size of a postcard
Gold & yellow flowers as the backdrop
Reminding the world of your Divinity
In fact, too beautiful for Earth
Your purpose far too great
That you must continue to exist in Spirit

Chloe Susan
Beautifully written in cursive
Your inked feet
A mother's most treasured memory
Just measuring over one inch
A visual I will cherish forever

The ankle bracelet, too big for you
Yet our connection in the hospital
Your last name
Baby Girl
2-5-19 @ 0330

A day & time
Forever burned
Into the depths of my existence

Your baptismal certificate
The only record of life

"Go therefore, & make disciples of all nations
Baptizing them in the name of the Father,
And of the Son,
And of the Holy Spirit."

Matthew 28:19

Your baptismal blanket
Hand-crafted & donated to the hospital
A grief experienced far too many times
It would appear

Created from someone else's wedding dress
A gift I had intended for you
As was also done for your sister

Made of silk
I rub my hands down
The front of what swaddled you
That night

Brushing the tips of my fingers
Over & over & over
The embellishments
Disrupting the flow
As this experience has done for my life

Laced in pearls
There is no irony
An emblem of the lunar cycles
The Divine sending you to me
This New Moon in Aquarius

A symbol of Venus

The goddess of love that emerges from the sea
Your birth moving the tides of my emotions
The mourning of Eve
As she is banished from Eden

The strings undone
Never retied after moving you for burial
I accidentally flip open
The cotton inside

Glazed with what lays
On all babies after birth
I rub my fingers
Feeling the gentle bump
At my fingertips

The pearls emerge from my eyes
As my dawn is in facing
This is the closest we will ever come
To touching one another
Again

Your crocheted white blanket
Emerges from the box
A deep inhale
Desperate for a smell
That reminds me of that night

The traditional blue & pink hospital blanket
The ultrasound pictures that remain
As I tossed your baby book
Impulsively wishing to pretend this never happened

A book to remember all those that came
Cards that were read once
And tucked away

Your little, white knitted cap
Too small for an American Girl doll
The hardest thing to touch
As I recall playing with the way it curled up

Just over your beautiful, face
A face, identical to Sophia's

Sisters, the perfect age gap
Never to be experienced
A memory of dolls & dress up
Bubble baths & matching outfits
Never to be witnessed

You see, the only memories I will ever have
Are the ones with you not in it
Yearning to see what it would have been like
To have two little princesses
That loved & adored their mommy so

To feel you, I must feel your death
As the final item of your memory box
A death certificate
Reminding me of the fleeting experience
Of being your mom

How many kids do you have?

If I say four
I open the doorway for awkward conversation
Sick of the way people look at me
That twisted look on their face
As if I am speaking a foreign language
Eyebrows furrowed
Horror in their eyes
Confusion on how to respond
Yes, I'm confused, too

A stillborn baby
Despite modern medicine
How is this still so common?

"It's okay"
I say
Attempting to comfort
Their discomfort

Why do I feel bad
That they feel bad
It's not okay
That I carry this loss

Beneath the surface of my conscious
Trembling
Like a volcano
Waiting for the slightest tremor
To release the pain
Oozing all over
Those around me

Would it just be easier to say I only have three children?

Can you hear me God?

This is my life
Trauma
More trauma
Will anything good ever happen for me?

I don't want to be powerless
I am tired of feeling lost
I know I have great purpose
Maybe in another lifetime
Just not in the cards for this one

It's time to trust
No more questions

How do I do that?
I fall to my knees in the shower
The pain hits me
A dagger in my heart
The betrayal of my own God
Hand over heart
I look up
The water splashing my face
Boiling hot
Burn this pain away

Are you there, God?
Do you see the pain I am in?
How could you watch while I suffer?
Why have you left me?
No one is ever there
Am I so unworthy
Even God doesn't love me?

The lump in my throat
Blocking my airway
Unable to breathe
Or make a sound

I move to lay against
The back of the tub
Holding my legs
Bracing the pain
My head between my legs

Radiating through me
An electrical pulse
Keeping me alive
While desperately wishing
I could just die

A sudden breeze brushes my arm

What was that?
It's so hot in here?

I swallow the last tear
I'm not alone
I will be
Protected
Guided

Grace always comes
That is the promise of the rainbow

God, Source, the Divine
This Higher Power
Watching
As we roam this realm
With complete amnesia
There must be more than this
A witness
On transmuting pain and suffering
Into healing
Into forgiveness
Into unconditional love
Compassion for humanity

As the water runs over me
The presence of something
Comforting me
The sobbing begins to slow
I can't tell what is tears
Or what is water

What I do know
Is the calm I feel
I feel something coming in
That will help me
To make sense
Of all of this

—

Chapter 3

"Goodbyes are only for those who love with their eyes. Because for those who love with heart and soul there is no such thing as separation."

Rumi

"We die many times in our lifetime."

Fragile
   Shattered
     Weak

Am I alive?
Or did I die with Chloe?
Her funeral wasn't the end
It was just the beginning

I haven't slept in almost a week
I can't sleep
I doze here and there
But no sleep
My sister gives me some pot
The night of the funeral
And I can finally let go

I have no idea where to start
A rose quartz crystal
A journal
Two books on death & bereavement

How can I feel so empty?
Yet so full of sadness, anger, bitterness, resentment, regret
It takes everything in me to get out of bed in the morning
A convincing text from Ryan that I need to try

The only thing that entices me is the cup of coffee on my
end table
I want to heal
I begin to scratch the surface of what I am feeling
The slightest bit of pain
Quickly replacing
 The band aid over my laceration

Is it 12 o'clock yet?
Asks the tequila sunrise
That reassures me

The pain will dissipate
I have the kids to distract me
I sit on the phone for hours
With my sister
With my friend Ava
Talking all things spiritual

How could God
Will the death of a child?
Most importantly
To an obedient Catholic
If the Church is the direct connection
To this powerful masculine energy

So many questions
Of why my life is
A story of pain & loss
The experience of joy
Always within arm's reach
Yet consistently slipping through my fingertips

Donnie doesn't know how to comfort me
He brings wine after work
A drunk wife
Seemingly working for both of us
My day centered around
Socially acceptable drinking times
If all mom's drink wine
I cannot be listed as an alcoholic

I don't know how to support Donnie
He is always silent
Busying himself with everything
Except being around

I always wanted four children
Am I a mother of four?
Or a mother of three
If I say the former
I open the door to discuss my dead child

If I say the latter
I neglect the child
I never got to know

Suddenly, a wave of grief hits
I run to the shower
My only solace in all of this
I sit on the floor of the shower
My hands to my heart
Rocking back & forth
Sobbing

What it would feel like to just hold her one more time.

A cool breeze, suddenly brushing up against me
In the steaming hot shower
Reminding me that
She is always near

Is the lesson to be had that death
Is only part of this infinite cycle
Connection maintained
At a multitude of levels?

"My schedule revolves around my next drink."

I have eight weeks to get it together
Before I have to return
To the questions that bombarded me
You had the baby?
Was it a girl or boy?
Let me see a picture of her!
It stirs a sickness in my stomach.

I sleep right until I have to get the kids ready
Completely exhausted
There is no baby keeping me awake all night
Just the haunting memory of her
3:30 a.m.
My body replaying the trauma
Each night
Each fucking night

My alarm sounds
I hit snooze over and over
Until I can't anymore
The kids need a mom

I can handle
Getting them dressed
I can handle
Getting them on the bus
But that's the extent
of what I can handle

Donnie brings Sophia to preschool
And I make my way outside in my robe
Dragging my feet
Following the path of devastation
From the night my water broke

Hovering the kitchen
Floating through the dining
Stepping down into the living room

Entering the door to my bedroom
Landing in the sunroom
Where it all began

I open those French doors
And step out into my safe haven
I sip my coffee
Light my cigarette
Staring out at the trees of my backyard
Unable to make sense of any of this

Logic is a fundamental part of this existence
And with this, there is none
Disbelief is my reality
My blank stare
A signal that I am barely present

Will I ever experience peace from this?

A couple of cigarettes later
I sloth back into bed
What do I do?
I look to my right
The grief & bereavement books
Sit on my end table

I look at one page
"How do you claim your own space for grieving?"
I slam the book down
I don't feel like I am grieving
I just feel numb

This book is useless
How could reading this fix anything?

I call my sister
I don't want to be alone
We talk for hours
About her Twin Flame
While I lay in bed
My legs tucked under my arms

It's a beautiful distraction
From my unshowered mess

By noon
I am trying to pull myself out
My kids will be home soon
I will have to get Sophia
They need their strong mama
Yet I feel like brushing my hair
Is the hardest task there is

It's time for a drink
I make a tequila sunrise
And I go back outside
I always need to be drinking something
When I smoke

Not wanting to smell like cigarettes
When I pick up the kids
I climb in the shower
And let the filth
Run off of me
How can we ever feel connected
When we hide the truth of our experiences?

Shame

The self-loathing
For not appreciating my pregnancy more
The regret
In not having faith that God would save both of us
The anger
That I can never catch a break in my life
The sadness
Over knowing my life will never be the same

This routine so robotic
Water aggravating my skin
As the droplets feel like
Hail amidst a thunderstorm

I stand there
The pressure penetrating
The barrier
My subconscious has created
To protect the devastation
Inside of me

My daily routine
      Cold
           Lifeless
                Lonely
                    Without purpose
        Drunk

"Unkept Promises."

I feel like I have already been
To the darkest places there are
Something in me says
"Don't go back."
I don't want to go back

About a month after Chloe's passing
My sister-in-law's baby shower is approaching
My childhood best friend
I promised her the day of the funeral
I wouldn't let this affect
My ability to love my niece

I broke that promise
I simply couldn't go
Sick with anxiety
Over the idea of being surrounded
By family & friends
The first time since the funeral

Preventing the somberness
From the loss of Chloe
Bleeding into
The celebration of her cousin

Just a month apart
They would have been best friends
Like their mamas

It's no surprise
Something so ideal
Would be ripped away from us both

Donnie called to let her know we wouldn't be going
She said she understood
But the calls and texts stopped coming after that

The void
Of who I was before Chloe
To who I am becoming
Affecting all of my relationships

Once a lover of family get-togethers
Extravagant holiday celebrations
Now consumed with sadness & misery

Barely able to change my clothes
Hair always in a bun
Unbrushed
No makeup
Lucky if I washed my face that day

Easter 2019 rolls around
From Donnie and I discussing filing for divorce
To agreeing to leave Easter lilies
At Chloe's grave

We head to his sister's house
To celebrate
The first holiday
Since Chloe's passing

I agreed to go
Despite the nausea
That kept me home from church
A sign of my subconscious
Communicating how I really feel

Sitting at the table
Everyone gets excited for my pregnant sister-in-law

The baby is kicking
And everyone can see it

I can feel the blood drain from my face
As I excuse myself to the bathroom
Trying not to make it obvious

Out of sight from everyone
I sprint
Only to find the door locked
What do I do now?

I head back to the table
Frozen
My hands are draped in my lap
I try to smile at my sister-in-law
Gently turning my head to Donnie
He immediately knows it's time to go
Telling his family
He suddenly doesn't feel well

As we pack up
Everyone hugs me
This silent understanding
Of the pain that radiates through my body
The trigger
Followed by the inability to escape

I decide that is the last family holiday
I will ever attend

How will I ever live again?

"When the grief finally hits."

Returning to work in April
What felt like spring renewal
After the devastating
Experience of winter

Trying to be as normal as possible
Dressing in suits
Styling my hair & make up
How can I expect people to understand
If I pretend to be okay?

Some of my clients
Had been informed
Prior to my return
Not everyone is a regular, though

Visibly not pregnant
The questions begin
One more time
Catalyst
A nervous breakdown
In the conference room
Across from my desk

Trigger after trigger
Unpleasant conversations
A sudden influx
Of pregnant women
Newborn cries
Flooding the waiting area of the bank

Rather than accommodate
My recent tragedy
The work begins to pile up
More responsibility
Trigger after trigger
Bitterness, resentment, anger builds

The only thing I have to look forward to

Is when Ryan comes to visit
The sound of his truck
Pulling into the driveway
A sound that triggers an excitement in my chest

Walking through the door with a sense of confidence
Observing his rugged, blue-collar look
An energy that radiates safety & security
Genuine in his interactions
He is the highlight of my work week

Clocking out
I race around to get the kids situated
With the only thing I truly look forward to
Being the bottle of wine
Sitting on my counter

I get the kids situated
Pour myself the first glass of wine
And head outside
To enjoy my after-work cigarette
Reminding myself that all moms drink wine

My thoughts are all over the place
Nothing really making sense
With the only conclusion
Affirming how unhappy I am
With no clear direction on how to change that

I smear the cigarette butt on my deck
Refusing to buy an ashtray
As I tell myself
Tomorrow
I will quit

Making my way towards the kitchen
I pour another glass of wine
To enjoy while I cook
Back to my normal routine
Maybe I can do this after all

That is
Until her first Christmas rolls around
Should we put a stocking up for Chloe?
The question returns
Do I have four children or three?

What picture do I put in the Christmas frame
When all I have are deceased photos of her
Photos only her mother can look at
Without cringing at the discoloration
That comes with a baby born in heaven

My sister-in-law sends a custom ornament
For Chloe's first Christmas
To remind us of why God called her back to Heaven
The thought was genuine, loving, and supportive
Yet, I ask Donnie to return it to her

I am not in a place to make peace with why this happened
As I desperately try to place blame
Consumed with anger
How this has changed my life
Change I never asked for
Or did I?

I begin to pull away from everyone
My friends cannot comprehend
As I fluctuate between trying to return to who I was
Without realizing she is gone

Pulling people in
Then isolating myself
Realizing how empty I am
Incapable of showing up
While facing daily triggers & mood swings

I don't need pep talks
Or reminders of how strong I am

"Tomorrow will be a better day"
"You will find meaning in this"

Throwing me over the edge
As someone refers to life after my miscarriage
She died at birth
Yet we can all relate
On the disappointment
Of going from
Living, breathing & growing
To earth-shattering loss

Seeing a mom post a reel on Instagram
Holding her baby that was born at 5 months
Just like Chloe
The mom had a faith
I must have lacked
Because her baby survived

Maybe if I throw the pregnancy book away
It will be as if nothing ever happened
Maybe if I box up all of her things
I can make this pregnancy disappear

It took eight months of triggers
A forced medical leave
A Christmas season
To drive home the grief
That I thought would never come
The grief everyone warned me about

Until now.

"My Soul Knows the Way"

Heal
The Universe decided
As I wake up one morning
Unable to walk
After trying to make the bed
The slipped disc in my back
Deciding today was the day
I would be bed ridden

July 2019
Now forced to sit in stillness
Not just facing the grief
But all of the feelings
I have been carrying
Over the course of the last few years

Chloe broke the lock
On Pandora's box
Outflowing the exiled parts of me
How one thing
Can suddenly illuminate how terrible
Everything is

I went back to my journal to again
Try to make sense of things
Just two weeks after she passed
I continued to see synchronicities
Affirming my life was moving in the right direction
Despite not being able to feel that way right now
My soul knew in this moment
That all of this was somehow aligned

I want to feel peace and love in my heart
I want a job working from home every day.
I want true, unconditional love in my life.
I want answers as to why my daughter died
I want justice in any means necessary
I want to be a yoga instructor & Reiki healer
I want to own my own holistic healing business

I want to help grieving mothers through my experience

Through my single experience
I realize the why
Is to help others find light in their darkness
But first
I must find my own

Through allowing myself to grieve
I find connection to Chloe
Once more
I want to experience her
Yet not the melancholy
How do I find joy
In this connection
When it was birthed in desolation?

Peace amidst chaos.

"Am I the victim or the villain?"

The power of the Sacred Feminine
Moves through me
Pushing back against the collective oppression
Defined by its limiting beliefs
Religion
Culture
Societal Roles

I have to consciously choose
To break free of this cycle
The spectacle removed from my eye
I begin to see the horror of what stares back at me

Awakening induced clarity
A sudden awareness as to
How hurt people hurt people
Am I the victim or the villain

Transformation cannot take place
Until I am willing to face
Myself
My choices
My fears
How they have shaped my relationships

Life molds the way we react
Sending us teacher after teacher
Until we are able to see
The betrayals, the lies
Reflections show the lack of self-love, self-respect
I carried within
Mirrors to the way I have also lied and betrayed others

Simply desiring to experience love
Yet not knowing what that means
Never knowing outside of a romance novel
That unconditional love & compassion is real

Caretaking my strength & my greatest weakness
"If I fix this problem for them, they will never leave."
It never works
Followed by my lashing out
As the void remains

"It is selfish to put yourself first."
My culture says
Begrudgingly serving my husband
Resenting my children that are draining the life from me
Serving others from an empty cup
My flesh deteriorating by the day
Resigning from the career I worked so hard to build
As I was simply exhausted

No longer knowing who I am
Moving through the motions of life
Settled with the loss of my Chloe

Things must be done differently
Which hard do I want?
To keep going through the motions of life
Fantasizing of experiencing the happiness
That seems to be out of reach

Or

Learn to think, feel & experience a life of joy
Radiating from within
Freeing myself of the conditioning
The judgment that flows from my wounded ego
Imprisoning the compassion of my spirit

No longer desiring to be numbed
By the ever-flowing red wine
Smothered in the smoke of my cigarette

"Mirror, Mirror on the Wall."

An escapist by nature
It is far easier to run
To blame others
Than to face the reality
Created by my codependency

It is far easier
To fixate on the problems of others
Than to recognize how big the problems in my life
Have become
A difference between awareness & accountability

How do I fix this?
How do I change this?

I ask the mirror
Unhappy with what I see
I pull out my journal
To remember what my soul bled onto its pages

I want to feel peace and love in my heart
I want a job working from home every day
I want true, unconditional love in my life
I want answers as to why my daughter died
I want justice in any means necessary
I want to be a yoga instructor & Reiki healer
I want to own my own holistic healing business
I want to help grieving mothers through my experience

The feelings of unworthiness
Replaced with the confidence of my love
For life & for humanity
Consciously choosing joy
Despite the pain this stirs

Choosing to rise from my own darkness
Rather than blame the world for my pain
The truth can finally rise up
Illuminating the path ahead
While not quite clear
I can feel in my heart space
The reminder
Everything always works out for me

How do we begin to see
the bigger picture of our experiences?
Surrender!
The nudge to take that class
That dream reminding you of a childhood passion

Randomly asking my Reiki practitioner
To certify me
The ad for a coaching certification
Leading me to become a Master Life Coach
A business selling bracelets
Transforming into leading people
As I myself heal

Each path followed
Validating the power of my intuition
Synchronicities reminding me
I am on the right path
Divine Guidance
Putting that smile on my face
When I feel like I am ready to give up

It is not easy to accept
That the loss of my child
Opened my heart
To the truth of who I was always meant to be
The truth of who I am

Opening my heart to healing
To show up in love
For myself
For my family

You cannot have joy, without knowing sadness
This human life
Full of chaos
Our spirit craving
The experience of joy
These lessons
Intended to teach us to strike a balance

"How can rebirth embody pain & pleasure simultaneously?"

Fear has halted me
Far too many times
From moving towards
My heart's desires
Believing deep down
What I wanted
Was always out of reach

Tired of feeling sad, angry, lifeless
Drowning in a bottle of Apothic
Slowly dying from each inhale of a coffin nail
Empowered to make a change
Fear slithering in like that of cyanide

Another reason to follow through
Begins the cycle
Into unhappiness
All over again

Stay in that unhealthy relationship
Walk away from that Masters Program
If you tell them how you feel
They will leave you

Do I really deserve this?
Am I even capable of such greatness?
Absolutely not
My fear reminds me

The chaos that stirs in my spirit
Instigates a tremble in my legs
Like a foal
Gaining her foot in the world

The movement of my spirit
A powerful catalyst for change
Activating at the soles of my feet
"You are fearless"

The innate creativity begins to stimulate me
"You are Divine, you are powerful"
She affirms
"Vulnerability, love, is your superpower"
She says
"Speak your truth"
As the bindings on my lips
Rip apart
One by one

I have no choice but surrender
Face the darkest aspects of who I have been
My experiences
What I have been through
Why I am
The way I am
The control that I have
In deciding what I want
To experience inner peace, love, & acceptance

What I don't want
To feel unworthy of love, of respect
To experience loneliness
Despite the presence of a lover

Affirming I want more for my life
I no longer fit in the confines of my space
Self-awareness leading me
The beauty, the value, that I am
Penetrating the confines
Of my chrysalis

No longer alone
I spread my beautiful, black wings
Expanding my reach
Beyond what the eye can see

As I connect with the spirit of the Divine
I am always supported
Separation an illusion
A power greater than me

Flowing through me

In the midst of my pain
I am able to see
How each experience
Has led me to this moment

Aligning me with purpose and
Teaching others to soar

With a heart cracked wide open
Tenderness oozing alongside
The abuse, the betrayals, the losses
I bleed for humanity
To feel the power that flows
Through each of us

"Will I ever experience peace?"

A conceptualizing society
We have become
Trying to organize every sentiment
Into a sense of logic
Failing to realize
Emotions connect us
To the spirit of our existence
Enlightenment

I often wonder
If the people who came up
With the stages of grief
Had ever lost a loved one

Five months to realize she was gone

The loss of a child feels more like
A pressure cooker
Mixing the emotions of
Sadness
Regret
Anger
Bargaining
Yearning
Hopelessness

It's not a cycle
But a blended experience
Of misery
Continuing until something happens

"Liam forgot his gloves for recess."
The snow is falling outside
The air so crisp, I have to make sure he has them
I just had a tequila sunrise

Not even wearing a bra

I jump in the car
To drop off his gloves

As I walk in
Blake is eating lunch in the office
He's struggling with his sister's death
I call Donnie to meet me at the school
Sweating bullets
Praying they can't smell
The alcohol on my breath
The cigarettes on my skin
We get in touch with a therapist for Blake

No one noticed

Close call
I have to stop drinking

The loss of a child
Goes against the rhythm of nature
My inner roadmap for safety
Attempting to provide me with
Every tool acquired
Over the course of my life
To cope with devastating emotions

Drinking
Smoking
Taking care of other people
Looking for jobs
Become a Life Coach
A Reiki Master
Start drawing again
Make friends
Stop talking to new friends
Crystals covering my body

Incense in every room
Journaling incessantly

Lavished with tools

"I am healed"
The world hears
"She is lying"
My spirit's muffled voice whispers
As I move through the cycles of caretaking
Avoidance behaviors to the pain of my reality

2020 goes by

Move a friend into my house
File for divorce

2021 goes by

Move another friend into my house
Fall in love
Try to push him away

Imposter syndrome
As I help people to heal
My perfectionism
Preventing me from seeing
How far I had in fact come

Processing grief
A nonlinear experience
Cannot be measured
Using a formula of logic
But through
The frequency
The duration
Of the triggered episode

Christmas 2021
My car breaking down
Just before Christmas Eve
The tow truck driver
Asking me how many kids I have
What their names are

Enough to trigger the grief

As I arrive home
The tears just keep flowing
I grab my soft, white blanket
Lay in my bed
And let this moment move through me

Giving permission to
The thoughts of Chloe to surface
Activating my heart space
There is a movement of love, rather than grief
I cry for the love I have for her
Rather than the loss of her

I miss you
I wish you were here
I wonder what your favorite toy would be this year
Laughing with Sophia by the tree
Your best friend
Forever to be
Your brother misses you so much
All that you have taught us
About the preciousness of life

The grief moves from my heart
Down through my stomach
The flutter of angst
Quickly passing

After moving through the experience
Of the sorrow
I call out for Ryan
"I just had an episode, but I am okay now."
Self-nurturance
Ask for support after
"What do you need from me?"
A partner that understands
Clarity over assumption
"Can you please hold me?"
And within minutes

He is there

My ego lied
Healing
Is like walking through fire
Burning away all that
Holds us back
A crimson process
With no promise
Unconditional positivity

"The Seasons of Grief."

Through all of this
I have come to realize
Healing is more
Like the passing of the seasons

Through the fall
I begin shedding the layers
Of thoughts and feelings
Carried through lifetimes
Catalyzed by the desolation of grief
In the loss of my beautiful daughter

The red, orange and yellow
Symbolizing the uprooting of my stability
Activating the spirit of my soul
Moving the feelings through my womb
And initiating the divinity within me

The harvest of the fall
Abundance experienced
Celebrating the release of my bondage
Only now able to experience alignment
With my most treasured loved ones
Ready to face the long, cold winter

The bareness of the trees
Covered in delicate snow
Purity blanketing the emptiness
From the fall harvest
A simple breeze
Moving the wet powder
Reminding us that change is ever-present

The days are shorter
The nights longer
The isolation of being confined
To sit with our experiences

Holiday after holiday
Reminding us of what is missing
The yearning begins to seep in
We experience the grief all over again
Longing for connection
The embracing warmth of touch
The reuniting kiss
Never to be had again
But held in the empty spaces
Left by tragedy

Will this period ever end?
Will the warmth of the sun ever penetrate my skin?
Will the renewal of love ever be part of my life again?
Is it possible to rise above the darkness?

A trip to Savannah, GA
To celebrate her third birthday
Inspired by new connections
That feel like the only ones I was ever meant to have

A strong embrace by the love of my life
Begins my day
February 5, 2022
A decision to do things different this year

A long, hot shower as I wash away the memories
That lead to this day
A birthday for a child I cannot touch
I cry, begging to have a day different than the rest

A bear hug from Ryan
Greeting me as I try to pull it together
We both cry
Thinking of the toll that this cycle takes on us both

He treats me to a couples massage
His family hosts a cookout
Always checking to ensure I am comfortable

A boat ride down the canal
Watching the sunset
Always inspiring to see how one color
Can omit so many shades

The wind whipping our faces
Winter is winter
No matter where you go
But the warmth of Savannah
Is to be had in the spirit of the people
Holding space for someone they just met
The evening ends
With a Chinese lantern
Surrounded by my newfound loved ones
Not so new, as I feel
They have always been with me
Held close by the mirror to my soul
"Happy Birthday, Chloe"

The days begin to become longer
The nights begin to shorten
The sound of birds outside my window
Signaling the snow to melt
Bringing warmth to the glooming grief

The first tulip
Beginning to bloom outside my door
It's yellow tips
Beginning to crack
The green, encompassing shell
The reward for maintaining hope

Excitement begins to stir
The shedding of despair
The desperation for connection
Filled by the warmth of the surrounding energy

Peace proposing a new chapter
Would you like to continue to cry
Over something you have no control

Or will you let me show you
That there is a promise of grace
Waiting just outside these doors

Inspired to step outside
The warmth of summer begins to empower
A desire to be surrounded by loved ones
Graduations
Baseball games
Birthday parties
Barbecues
Vacations

Once avoided at all costs
Now embraced by the healing in my spirit
Watching Sophia's Kindergarten graduation
Sitting next to Donnie
Our daughter able to experience the love
Both her parents have for her
Without looking to what direction
She should run first

Forgiveness, compassion, grace
Blanketing us both
As we both realize
Hurt people, hurt people

The spirit of Source
Using us to teach those around us
That camaraderie is possible
Post-divorce

Tears begin to roll down my face
The sudden ache realizing that Chloe would be three
Sitting in my lap watching her sister
Sing the ABC's of Kindergarten
Unable to stop
I am grateful for the sunglasses over my face

Another missed milestone
The grief still sits

Despite the resounding heat of summer

Collapsing onto my bed
I stare up at the ceiling
Realizing I have been holding her spirit hostage
"It is time to let go."
I place my hands over my chest
Knowing the pain that is about to ensue

I exhale the ache that still holds space
Guilt that I was still holding on so tight to
"Let it go"
Letting go doesn't mean I have forgotten her
Letting go allows me to fully appreciate
That as one of my children
She brought me closer
To who I was always meant to be

The seasons move through cycles
Much like the grief experienced in life
A promise of better days
Always present, only to be valued

Through the passing of the seasons

Chapter 4

"Love sees roses without thorns."

German Proverb

"To Experience Love, We Must Let Go."

For ten years
I blamed him
I blamed Donnie
For everything that happened to us
Never feeling what he had done was enough
To make me happy
But what he didn't do
Created the pain of my very existence

Over the course of my journey
After Chloe
Finally understanding

The only one who can victimize me
Is me
The only one who can make me happy
Is me
The only one who can foster overflowing love
Is me

Up to this point
I didn't understand
The boundaries I lacked
Misunderstanding my own needs
Trusting I will receive it
Learning to let go
Incorporating forgiveness
As I come to realize fully
That perfection is impossible to attain

I began to explore this
During our marriage
As I attempted to heal from Chloe
Desperately trying to find happiness
Peace & contentment

Pushing me inward
More & more
Only further driving home

The need for us to part ways

Our foundation built on a trauma bond
A fantasy of marrying someone from childhood
My best friend's brother
Yet, beneath the shell of what the world saw
Was fruit that had rotted away
Left out amidst roaring summer heat
Produced by the passion of our energies

An enmeshment
No clear understanding of where one began
And the other ended
Society teaches this is healthy
An obsession & complete devotion
To one another
Psychology calls it codependency

Caretaking
Control
Low self-esteem
Repression of feelings
Obsession over other's behaviors
Controlling as fear of losing control takes over
Denial of problems
Poor communication
Weak boundaries
Lack of trust
Anger
Inability to connect sexually
Lethargy
Depression
Hopelessness

A rediscovery of self
Necessary to move beyond this
To think that the desire for human connection
Can produce that type of experience

Both coming from
Abusive & neglectful backgrounds

Best intentions to create a life opposite of that
Subconsciously bringing forward
All of the behaviors utilized
To survive the things that have happened to us

You see…
There is no villain in any break-up or divorce
Just two souls
Constrained by the wounded ego
Battling to be right

When the answers to the problems are
In the name of love

Once the villain of my story
Now a lesson for my healing path
As I accept the role
I played
In the chaos of my home

I was angry all the time
From not honoring myself
Not working to heal
Instead drinking my days away
Isolating myself

Unsatisfied by any material item
Bought or given to me
Surpassing success in all things I did
Beautiful, healthy children
All because the concept of martyrdom
Settling for the best I thought I could do
Was the roadmap of my life

The easiest divorce the judge had ever seen
Enough love & compassion
To accept
That we are healthier apart

A life full of purpose
Engaged & present with myself

Painting through my feelings
Drawing to challenge myself
Reading to heal myself
Gardening to balance myself

Adventuring with my children, my love
Making amends & forgiving others
A life fully lived
Not driven & inspired by
Money
Outward appearances
Success
Perfection
Rather
Moment to moment

Showing up for myself
A pivotal role in my experiences with others
Saying no when I mean no
Confidently turning down things not meant for me
Communicating my likes & dislikes appropriately
Bringing balance to the things I do
Surrendering the need to be perfect
Recognizing all the good in my life
Rather than fixating on what is perceived to be missing

Through this journey
I transform from the inside out
A cellular remodeling
Not void of pain
Transforming me into Ashley Sapphire
Almost unrecognizable
As I approach life differently
Carrying myself with compassion & grace

The more we work at this
The more effortless it becomes
To face adversity
To face those still consumed by their pain

The veil of the wounded ego
Suppressing their soul
We pray for them
To find healing
Rather than condemning them to more pain

There are no villains in this story
Just those who signed up
To play this role
On your healing journey
To become closer to God
In this lifetime
And the following

"An Activation of True Love."

Life isn't ever going to be
Simple
That much I have come to understand

We would never be able to experience
The rainbow
If it wasn't for the flooding
Of the storm

All I had to do
Was surrender
Anchored my roots to the safety of Gaia
A bright, white light
Flowing freely through my roots

Purifying my physical body
As it swirls through
Every last inch
Of my human existence

A deep exhale
Ushering out any & all thoughts
That don't align with
My new vision for life

Visualization
Recovered through my healing journey
Allowing me to connect
With the loss of creativity
That comes with trauma

Creativity is the sword
We take to battle each day
Navigating the chaos
Of this earthly life

A feeling of peace
Now covering me

Like the warmth of the sun
Pressing against one's face
A sense of reprieve on a cold, winter day

There is something about how
The snow just won't stop
That reminds me of him

Even when I look around
And allow the illusion of his absence
To let me believe that I will never him again
I feel him stronger than ever

As I look at the snow
I hear him promise
I am coming back to you
But I, too, must surrender
Surrender to the timing
Having faith that all things happen
Just as the snow falls each winter

Reminiscing on each time
We crossed paths
The oddity of thinking of him
Then suddenly watching him appear
Two souls
Sharing in one experience
An infinite cycle of love
Unknowingly
Restoring my faith
In a power greater than I

It's okay to be scared
This kind of love
Requires vulnerability

Self-acceptance
A mirroring of faults & failures

He the sun

I the water
Nourishing the seed
That grows beneath the surface
A seed planted by the Universe
To bring two souls together
In pure love

As I watch the snow fall
I admire the way it drapes over the trees
A soft, white blanket
Accenting the dreariness of winter
Reminding me of the way
We accent one another

An eternal love
That will faithfully flow
As the river always does
Effortless
In the face of the one
Your heart will bleed for
Over & over

Love does not claim
But…
I am yours
You are mine
God's promise
To us

The rainbow after the storm.

"Making Amends"

I stand in my hotel room
Shocked by my reality
Hosting a women's retreat
Here
In Sedona, AZ

These women
Inspired by me
Are here to be close to me
To experience what I offer
Through a business
Founded in the loss of Chloe

As I prepare to hike the day
Over the red rock
I reflect on my growth
Less than a year ago
Completely unmotivated to do anything
Now eager to explore the world

My friend comes running into my hotel room
Her mom had sent her the new Adele song
"Easy on Me"
My soul trembles
As the volcano is awakened
The feelings I have surrounding myself
As a mother
The guilt I carry
The shame
Of wishing
I could turn back the clocks of time
Suddenly erupting to the surface

19 years old when I had Blake
A complete mess, but desperately trying to find my way
Changing my life forever
Through him, I grew up
Not realizing the transfer of energy

As I found consolation in his snuggles
Affected him subconsciously
Developing the anxiousness of
Needing to keep others happy
As he grew older
All I ever desired
Was to give my kids more than I had
A safe environment
Never worrying about the unexpected

A place to come home to
Two parents that loved them dearly
A belief that kept me in a marriage
That shouldn't have made it to the altar

Only to realize I hurt them in other ways
Drowning in a bottle
To cope with the loss of Chloe
To avoid facing the hard work
That my marriage illuminated

"You weren't there for me for the last 3 years!"

A fight that almost pushed him
To leave me
The worst it had ever gotten
But I was there
Or so I thought
How do you show up emotionally
For your children
When you are barely hanging on by a thread?

Ryan saved my life
The bond piecing me back together
Fusing the boundaries with
Love
Compassion
Grace
Simplicity
Appreciation
A regret in not meeting him sooner

Quickly rebounded with the realization
I wouldn't have Blake, Liam, Sophia or Chloe
Everything happening as it is meant to
However painful it felt at times

"You were just angry all the time."
Liam tells me as we sit on the beach
Our first time together in almost a year
"Was I a good kid at all?"
He asks
My heart shattering into a million pieces
Realizing how I had made him feel
I struggled to do my best
Amidst the cards that our family was dealt

"You were more of a mom than my own"

Perplexed over his anger for me
Abandoning him during the divorce
Not going to a single baseball game
Changing his bedroom

How do I tell him
I was walking a fine line
Between fighting for time with him
And being reminded he wasn't biologically mine?
To stare at another empty room?
The feeling of losing two children?

I choose to let him vent
To blame me
To lay out every feeling he ever had
Rather than justify my actions
I give him the space he so desperately needs
To feel heard & seen

You see…
That is the thing
As justified as we feel in our actions
Unreciprocated by another
So doesn't another person

Part of healing
Is simply learning to hold that space
Honoring the person we love & cherish

One gift I always desired to give my kids
Was the trust to tell me
The truth of what they feel
To fix it & create a safe space for them

As Mothers
As parents
Do we ever escape the shame & the guilt
That comes with providing for our children?
Will we ever get this right?

The Divine using my friend
To trigger me
Just before a hike
Intended to help me
Release
Heal
Align
As is why we are in Sedona

Part of healing
Is recognizing the ways in which
Our survival mechanisms
Developed through our traumas
We in fact hurt others
To make amends where able

The loss of Chloe
The feeling of failing her
By my lack of blind faith
That God would save us both
Had I stopped the labor
Opening the door
Seeing through clearer eyes
What my children truly needed
A present mother

An engaged mother
Not a *perfect* mother

I will spend the rest of my days making it up to them.

—

"A New Perspective on Healing"

We see this image portrayed online
That the healing journey
Of love & light
Is as simple as reciting daily affirmations
Believing that we are worthy of great things
That life is more than our experiences

Reminding me of the feeling that is stirred
By looking through a magazine like <u>Cosmopolitan</u>
Comparing their looks to brushed images of supermodels
Smeared across the page
Never feeling like the goal of being more is attainable

If we tell our brain that life is as simple & beautiful
As the ease of the sun rising
After the darkest of nights
We negate not only the years of conditioning
But the very human emotions
That come with the uncomfortable experiences in life

If facing ourselves was as simple
As opening our eyes to the awareness
Of the sun rising
Everyone would simply do it

They wouldn't be reaching
For their next drink
Their drug of choice
Bouncing from relationship to relationship
Shaming themselves because
They can't get out of this
Chaotic loop

Life will never be absent of painful experiences
We must allow ourselves to be cracked open
Like a coconut in which the ego releases its grip
Embracing that despite the discomfort
This moment is part of the present
Aligning us with what is in fact meant for our spirit

Through facing ourselves
How our choices have affected us
We choose to rise up
Rather than wither away in the shame
We choose to fight for our happiness
Until it comes so natural
We can face a situation
Internalizing the peace we wish to experience
As we face the storms that rage around us

A belief so strong
As we remember our roots
That we are worthy
That we are deserving
That we are so much more
Than the things that have happened to us
The things that may happen to us

We move beyond fear
Allowing vulnerability
Occasionally closing off at the presence of danger
Simultaneously remembering how in the past
That we have survived what we thought would once kill us

The dam around the heart
Now removed
Facing the reality
Of the ruins left by the hurricane
With no choice left
But to rebuild
A world that we wish to experience
What greater gift than
To start with a clean slate

In facing how our choices have affected us
We see how they have hurt others
The once perceived villain
Easier to understand
As we seek the same
Understanding & compassion

From others

We show up through changing our behaviors
Not just saying we will

Healing is a journey
An act of moving from one place to the next
Not a destination
As we allow ourselves to move beyond
Our suffering
Our desires created by the ego
We embrace that we are more than just this self
No longer separate from others
Through difference of beliefs, choices, experiences
Part of a greater collective
All desiring an experience of unconditional love &
compassion

"The Concept of Forgiveness"

January 2022
Estranged from my father for two years
A disagreement initiated by my decision to get a divorce
Came as no surprise
As the limiting beliefs I was breaking from
Were fostered through my upbringing & culture

Through my healing
I had embodied the concept
That I owe nobody an explanation for my decisions
A difficult pill for others to swallow

A courtesy text
To let me know that his brain tumor had returned
He was to have surgery at the end of the month

Nonetheless
An argument ensued
As I held my ground
A battle to be right between the two egos
A challenge for those with a newfound sense of
empowerment
The boundary standing tall like a brick wall

I decided the most I could commit to
Was sending him a card
To let him know I was thinking of him

Then came the day of his surgery

The sudden realization
That I may never see him smile at me again
Or the sound of his voice a distant memory
Shocked me awake
Frantically Facetiming him
I was too late

As he had just been wheeled off to surgery
I laid in bed
Frozen in fear
The embers that had been slowly burning
Now producing full flame heat
As the self-hatred flows through me
For allowing my pride to get in the way

After everything I have been through
After all of the work I have done
How did I fall back into this space
The need to be right
To dig my heels in
Punish this man for all that he had done
Decades ago
Allowing the past to rule this present moment

Failing to integrate
How trauma & stress
Had influenced how I showed up as a mother
Meanwhile I condemn this man
For how he showed up as a father

"Just give me one more chance to see my dad"

I plead with God
I tried this before & failed
But something inside told me to try again

I promised that I would finally let go
Of all that he had done
Accepting that none of us are perfect
We do the best with what we know in that moment
Adult children carrying the pain of the past
The human condition embodies self-preservation
One that none of us are exempt from

Now finally understanding
What it means to be on the other side of that coin
As a parent doing the best she could

With the cards she was dealt
Applying this compassion
Choosing forgiveness
For one more chance to hear his voice

"I love you, dad."
"I love you, too."

Forgiveness
Whether we decide to rekindle that fire or not
Is for us, not the other person
By allowing the release of bitterness & resentment
We clear space for the experience of unconditional love
Through ourselves & with others

"More Hurdles to Navigate"

It was supposed to be my last mammogram
Feeling confident & hopeful
A hop in my step
Courageously asking Ryan to focus on work
I can handle this one myself

"The doctor would like to speak with you before you go"

Perplexed, I tilt my head to the side
Squinting at the radiology technician
Unable to utter a word
I whisper, *"Okay"*

*"Considering your family history & the changes we are
seeing, it's time to do a biopsy of these areas."*

An ancestral curse
Attacking all that is feminine
No stone unturned
As I too shall face the same demise

The irony of this happening
While publishing my first book
A book about finding peace amidst chaos

As I stare at the doctor
Tears begin to roll down my face
I stare blankly ahead
Gripping the sides of my hospital bed
My legs crossed at my ankles
I begin to feel the sweat between them
As I clench them tighter & tighter

Why can't I simply just catch a break?
Almost on the other side of the pain of Chloe
Where more days feel fulfilled than empty
The Universe delivering yet another problem

Will I ever have a period where life just flows?
Going down the rabbit hole of negativity
The doctor is talking
I am no longer listening
As my brain begins to process the idea of having breast
cancer
At just 34 years old

"The nurse will call to schedule the biopsy."

I try calling Ryan, but he doesn't answer
Normally a trigger of abandonment
I remind myself he is working
I lean into my best friend Kayley

She reminds me that regardless of outcome
I have the best-case scenario
It was caught so early
As she says this
My love no sooner calls
To remind me of the same thing

I am able to take a deep breath
Wipe the tears away from my face
Giving gratitude for the Divine guidance
That led me to early screening
A support system
That I can trust & rely on
An internal map of safety
That validates me from within
It is in these moments
That we lean into previous experiences
To empower ourselves through life's challenges

I reflect on how I survived
The tragic loss of my daughter
Something I thought would be the end of me
I reflect on how I survived
My divorce
Something I feared doing for so long
Yet unfolded naturally & effortlessly

As I applied much of what I learned
Through my healing journey
The power to shift energy through influence
Unconditional love & compassion
Embodied through the surrendering of judgment

Fear an illusion
Blind faith the magic carpet
Leading us to our destiny
While unable to see how this serves me
I trust that it will
As it always has before

Chloe a gift
Like all of my children
Teaching to be that of blind faith
How something so tragic
Could align me
With healing
With purpose
This situation
To be no different

I take a deep breath in
"We will figure it out & get through this."
Ryan says
For the first time in my life
I feel those words to be true

"Love, the Cherished Emerald"

Like a phoenix
Emerging from the ashes
I honor the place I have come from
Devotion to my journey
Gratitude becoming the
Only prayer I speak

In the wake of my healing
I stopped denying
The pain that I permitted
The abuse I inflicted on myself

Neglect of my needs, my desires
Lack of self-love
Lack of self-respect
All from living in fear of change
Never believing I was worthy
That all that I have now
Was nothing more than a long, lost dream
Tragedy the key to the door of my awakening

I have dreamt of this moment
Too many times to count
Engraving my prison walls
The tally marks of days gone
Never realizing I had the power to free myself
Until now

True love was never separate from me
The breaking of my spirit
Gave space for God, the Divine
To move through me

To experience something new
We must release the ways of the old
One cannot pour the lusciousness of love
In the same pan containing the brick of
Melted bitterness, anger, self-loathing
Expecting the experience of joy

To be penetrable & everlasting

To clear space requires
Trials & tribulations
Tragedy
Loss
Trauma
Knowing the outcome
With absolute surety
We would never surrender into the lesson unfolding

Affirming, I am love
An overflowing dam
Full of compassion & grace
Self-forgiveness bringing forth
Total understanding

No more hiding behind
Denial
Self-deprivation
Shame

Consciously replacing with
Daily meditation
Personal space
Honoring heavy feelings
Balance in what I love most

Through awareness of my self-imprisonment
I feel what awaits me
Just outside my prison door
The missing puzzle piece
All of what my heart aches for

Ryan smiling back at me
Saying…

You are free.
You are loved.
You are safe.
You have won.

We made it, Ashley.

"A Love Like This"

Tears of gratitude
As I recall what I went through
To reach this moment
A vast sense of appreciation
Consuming my body

A tingling sensation moves through me
From head to toe
Assured that
Things are the way
They are meant to be

Every aspect of my life
Once stripped away

Physically
Through the loss of my child
Ten years in banking
Down the drain
An 'unimaginable' divorce

Emotionally
Learning that my happiness stems from within
That I have the right to pursue my needs first
Taking the time to process
What saddens me
What angers me
Allowing the true gift of grace to move through me

Mentally
Facing the low self-esteem
That has been driving my decisions for years
Never believing I was worthy
Of what my soul truly desired

A life of peace
A life full of experiences
Sitting at the beach
Hand in hand

Gazing at the Full Moon
In absolute silence
The sound of waves crashing
Against the rocks
My head on the shoulder
Of the love of my life

Pushing my daughter on the swings
Listening to her laugh
Telling me today is the best day ever
Watching my son play football
Telling me about his dreams of playing at Clemson
Long hikes with Autumn

A life full of laughter, of love
My soul calling out amidst my distress
The way in which Juliet calls out for her Romeo
Somehow, the pain of all that loss
Calling in everything I ever wanted

The love flowing through me
The antidote to my miserable existence
Filling the space of what once was
Love finding its way to me
Despite the loss of all I once thought
I couldn't live without

I close my eyes
Placing my hand over my heart
As it feels like it could explode at any moment
Lips beginning to quiver
As I allow myself to feel the flutter in my spirit

I'll always remember that first moment
When we realized we were in love

Absolute awe of one another
As if time simply stood still
And we were the only ones in existence

I had stopped to see him at work
The sun was shining so brilliant behind him
Rays of yellow, and gold, beaming down as he smiled at
me
His face always so bright when he sees me
That smile conveys so much love for me

A genuine and gentle man
So full of love and compassion for others
I move in for the hug that declares
You are safe with me.

As I stand there
Remembering
I breathe in deeply
Recalling the comfort
The smell of his after shave
Combined with the grittiness of his day
The scent permeating his love & protection

I move back into the memory
Drawn back to his eyes
Their softness
Gives an unspoken signal of trust

I feel seen, heard, validated
Ryan always catches me staring at him
His eyes are so light
Hazel with a touch of green

Complete disbelief
We found each other
Billions of people in this world
And I found mine

Complete disbelief
That a love this profound exists
When you endure what we've endured
It's hard to fathom
Life exists beyond trauma

"I think I'm in love with you, Ryan."
"I love you"
He responds

And for the first time
I am with someone
Who truly means it

I feel the energy move through me as I recall that moment
I always feel this way around him
A tingling sensation throughout my body
Suddenly calming my nerves

Being near him
Brings me to a place of balance
In the way an extended meditation would
A balanced, harmonious, supportive love
Fostering connection, safety, and a sense of peace

His love the switch to my soul
Reminding me of the light inside
The missing puzzle piece
That I have spent decades searching for

I deserve to be loved this much
Putting the pain & suffering behind me
Integral to aligning with this new timeline
One full of love, joy, & peace

My thoughts shifting
To the way he reaches out his arms
For me to sit with him

There is something about
Climbing into his lap
And curling up to his chest
That allows for me to completely let go
I experience deep relief
In aligning with peace in my life
Never able to get close enough to him
Always nudging closer to his chin

Him immediately pulling me closer
Gently placing his hand on the small c
Of my back

My gentle giant
The pressure of his fingertips
As he, too, can't get close enough

The smell of his work clothes
The experience of home
Within another person
He is everything
I have ever prayed for in a man
Loving me like no one else ever could
The only one who knows how

What more could I expect
From my twin soul
Everything about us is mirrored
The pain
The trauma
The way we experience life
The way we desire to love & be loved

"I am Grateful for it all."

Gratitude is the key
Catalyzing movement
Change within one's character
Dispelling all things negative

There is pain in giving gratitude
For abuse
For grief & loss
For chaos

The ego wanting to scream
This is unfair!
Why would I ever sign up for this shit!
How is it okay that another person hurt me?

Acceptance is not giving permission
For these things to happen
It is restoring power
In the moments where we feel absolutely powerless

There is no joy
Without acceptance
As there is no breaking dawn
Without the darkness of the night
The void that allows for us
To go within
Exploring the depths of our soul
Connecting us to the infinite experience
Of this vast universe

One moment at a time
Easing into the understanding
That the past no longer
Holds the weight of
These pages down

Pages liberating the

Blood, sweat, tears
Of these last three years

Compassion in the face of adversity
Angels & guides clearing the path ahead
The headlights on a dark night
Guiding the path home
Revealing only that of which
Is required to be seen

Anger
The check engine light
Illuminating the negative thoughts
Steering me off path
The spirits way
Of saying
"You deserve better"

Self-judgment
Inferiority
Seeing others as perfect
A rabbit hole
Of self-sabotage

A sudden movement
Reminding me to keep my eyes
On the road ahead
I can rest when I get to my next stop
Grabbing on to the things
That remind me of
My awesomeness

A motivational book
A butterfly in the corner of my eye
The sound of a raven above me
A smile from Ryan
A hug from my children
A text from a client
Reminding me how I changed their life
All in perfect timing
Reminders that I am

Where I am supposed to be
An infinite experience of love
Always in & around me
I am grateful for it all

A once tired soul
A belief that I was damaged goods
Transmuted through the fire
Into my birthright of
Joy
Peace
Contentment
The things that once mattered
Replaced with the right to feel & experience life
The way I desire to

Love
Once something I thought I had to earn
Emotionally unavailable parents
As they navigated the stresses of life
The root of their own traumas
Buried beneath the surface
Erratic & unpredictable behaviors
Shunning emotional reactions
Passing the torch in ancestral wounds
Now carried in my breasts
Contained
Soon to be removed
I am grateful for it all

People pleasing
Control
Perfectionism

A continuation of healing
Illuminated through my anger
A milestone in healing
As I learn to transmute it creatively
Detaching from the world
Allowing it to move through me
In its truest form

Of disappointment, sadness, grief
I am grateful for it all

Surrendering into this life I manifested
The absence of time
Less focus on productivity
More on living
My right to flow
With the river of life
I am grateful for it all

Recognizing the need to shift
From victimization to empowerment
Through acknowledgment of
The pain within another soul
Projected onto us
Through their own behaviors
Despite how painful it may be

Embracing the lesson that comes
In mirroring our own behaviors back to us
Allowing myself space & detachment
In accepting I am powerless
Over other's expectations & opinions of me

I am grateful for it all

"The Winding Road Home"

As I pull into the cemetery
The judgment immediately begins
"I can't believe it's taken you this long to visit."
"What kind of mother doesn't go to her daughter's grave?"

I drive up the long road
Veering to the left
Making a hook shape
In the path to my daughter

Her grave sits on top
Of her pop pops
Highlighted by the tallest
Gravestone in the entire cemetery
11/11
Her pop pop's birthday
Reminding me of the Divine orchestration
Of all of this

A dirt path off of the road
Allows for me to park
At the base of the hill

My hands on the steering wheel
Beginning to sweat
As a I hold on for dear life
My heart sinking into my stomach
Knowing what waits for me
At the top of that hill

I avoid this trip
As I cannot do it
Without a burst of emotion
Perpetual sobbing
A burst that turns to
Complete exhaustion
A puffy face
A need for a nap
Take out
And garbage TV
Sobbing convulsively
As I did
2/9/2019

It has taken me three years
To muster the courage
To decorate her grave
An act of acknowledgment
That says she is dead
An act of acknowledgment
That I will never see her again
A judgment my ex-husband would remind me of
Each birthday that passed
Compassion as I know he simply
Doesn't understand

A truth I now feel ready to face
As I drive the first stake into the ground
Two black planters
A space to hold the flowers
I intend to bring
On a regular basis

Her stone, a marker in the ground
A baby angel on the left
Her name across the stone
Placing a pink tricycle
As her gift
A gift to remember that this year
She would have been learning to ride one

Alongside her sister
As I sit there on my knees
Ryan's hand gently placed
Behind my shoulders
I pray for peace
Surrounding her loss

Peace is the freedom we give ourselves to be present
The belief that we can do the things we desire
Or to pursue what brings us resounding joy
A gift that Chloe has given to me
Breaking me free of the matrix
As her tragic death
Shook me awake
Falling asleep at the wheel of life

She gave me the freedom to feel
The wind whipping against my face
Forced to close my eyes
Trusting this man
To lead the way on our journey

A peace that comes with sitting in the unknown
A place of transition
Accepting that all is as it should be
A Chloe tattoo putting a smile on my face
Reminding me of this concept
Rather than tail spinning me
Into an episode of grief
A reminder of where I started
To where I am now
Internal knowing that she is
In & all around me

The sun blazing on my back
As I lay on the back of the boat
Listening for hours
To the sound of Ryan fishing

Experiencing for the first time in my life
A connectedness to all things

A passing storm
A beautiful sunset
A shared kiss
Resting ducks
The warmth of the sun
The anchoring mud

She gave me the freedom
To connect with her siblings
Through my own healing
A healing that stemmed from her death

Running outside
To snap a picture of the double rainbow
As Sophia jumps up & down
"Look, mama, look!"

The everlasting promise that comes
With learning to let go
And letting God, the Universe, a Higher Power
Move in & through you

Unconditional Love
Compassion
Grace
Peace
Joy

This is what Chloe has given me.
Has given *you*.

Epilogue

It would only make sense
Amid the writing of this book
I would face another trauma

Another attack on my femininity
An infection of my uterus
Taking the life of my infant
An ancestral wound
Traveling to the heart of my breasts
Calling for their painful removal

A testament to the story written here
Life never being absent
Of…challenges
Of…obstacles
Of…uncomfortable feelings

The journey is in
Aligning to the purpose
Behind the madness
Finding the peace
Amid the chaos

Despite this next phase
Involving a double mastectomy
Feelings of unfairness surface

How many things must
I continue to go through?

Oh, how far I have come
To find the silver lining
Not giving up on my dreams
Leaning into the love of my partner
Surrendering to the help of others
Embracing the present moment
More than ever

A powerhouse of women's issues
Fostering union during diversity
Miscarriage versus infant loss
Preventative surgery versus breast cancer

All united through
The heartache & grief
Of life's experiences
Brought together
Through hope
Greater understanding
Collective healing

So begins the next journey of healing in this lifetime...

About Ashley Sapphire

Ashley Sapphire, owner of Healing of the Divine Rose, is a certified Reiki Master/Teacher, Certified Master Life & Spiritual Coach, and holds a BA in Spanish Education & Psychology.

Ashley's passion for coaching people began in her ten year banking career, where she held a variety of leadership roles, managing people, as well as major bank projects. Through the tragic loss of her daughter Chloe in 2019, the direction of her life work shifted towards a role in leading people through their darkest moments, learning to find peace and purpose amidst the chaos!

Ashley's charisma for life naturally empowers clients to not just want more for themselves, but to do more! Compiled with her attention to detail and highly intuitive nature, she never misses a beat with a client, tailoring each session to meet their needs. As being human is far more complex than reciting affirmations, doing daily exercise, and praying for a miracle, Ashley covers in her program the layers of being human, how our development plays a role in our connection to ourself and others, but most importantly how to align to our innate desires through personal accountability. Her program prompts the client to access their inner source of wisdom, resilience and growth, thus aligning them with their highest potential through entelechy (the channel through which this manifests).

You may learn more about Ashley's programs and offerings on her website, www.divinerose.net.

Make sure to follow her on all of her social media platforms (@ashley_sapphire_official), where you will experience an abundance of content to guide you on your healing journey!

Made in the USA
Middletown, DE
07 October 2022

12217120R00099